WRITERS REPUBLIC

# MY TWO FATHERS

ELVIRA THOMAS

**WRITERS REPUBLIC L.L.C.**
515 Summit Ave. Unit R1
Union City, NJ 07087, USA

**Website:** *www.writersrepublic.com*
**Hotline:** *1-877-656-6838*
**Email:**  *info@writersrepublic.com*

Ordering Information:
Quantity sales. Special discounts are available on quantity purchases by corporations, associations, and others. For details, contact the publisher at the address above.

Library of Congress Control Number:        2021931923
ISBN-13:              978-1-63728-142-0      [Paperback Edition]
                      978-1-63728-143-7      [Digital Edition]

Rev. date: 03/30/2021

# Awards and Recognitions

In recognition of Coach Livi (Olivia S Anderson) who spoke the Word of God in my life, telling me the Lord said I should write a book. Being uncertain, she encouraged me to complete the assignment the Lord had given me.

# Dedication

With deep gratitude and honor to my daughter Trisha, who encouraged and supported me as I had to relive the past and the pain of my childhood. I refer to her as my psychologist as she patiently listens to my fears and concern. She saw my strength and minister to me like the Woman Of God she truly is.

# Contents

---

# Introduction

"Lord, please, are You hearing me? Could you come down here right now? I am so scared, Lord. Why does this always have to happen? We didn't do anything to deserve this kind of treatment or punishment. So much tension, so much stress. Everyone is nervous and on edge. You could feel the tension in the air, in the atmosphere. We are walking around on needles. Look at us, and You will see the fear, the desperate need for a way of escape."

As a child, this was my daily prayer. I lived with that fear and torment, all the way into my adult life. I could not seem to get away from it, no matter how far I ran, no matter where I hid, no matter how much I pretended.

# Part 1

---

## My Earthly Father: Daddy

I grew up on a small, beautiful island in the West Indies, but my childhood was anything but beautiful. As I reflect, I can see the roller coaster of emotions and pain that I lived through. It seemed like a never-ending cycle of violence. I was always crying out to God to protect and save us from what was a nightmare. We were always pounced on. We were the object of his unprovoked anger. I walked on pins and needles. I hated my life. I was torn between loving and hating my father. Yes, this was all at the hands of my father.

I would look up at the sky, trying to see beyond the clouds, and cry out to God, "God, You seem so far away. Can You hear me? Here I am, Lord, sitting here by myself. Can You see me? Lord, why is this happening to us? Can You protect us? Can You send your angels to be here with us? Can You do something, Lord? I know You are a big God, and I believe You, so please do something about this situation before it blows apart right now." I prayed like this often.

Growing up, we seldom went to church, but my father never missed a Sunday. It was important that we learned certain biblical principles. The Bible was taught in school where I learned about a God who watches over us, who know everything, and loves us unconditionally. When we are scared, we can call on Him, so that is what I did. Prayers were said in school upon admission and dismissal. As I saw it, Jesus Christ, the son of God, our Lord, and Savior, was the main character in the New Testament so this is where most our teachers taught from. Learning the commandments was also a big priority. Yes, it was interesting to learn about God and Jesus and what happened when they are a part of your life, but that did not mean my relationship with Him was personal.

As a child my relationship with God was based on what I was taught. At school, the Word of God was a major subject and prayers were said before and ending of school. I learned to believe in a God I could not see, to fear Him, and call on His name. I asked or begged Him for things my mother could not provide for us. I knew the Lord's Prayer early on. My siblings and I had to say it every night before bed and on awakening. Any other prayer was said quietly, private prayers to God, secret prayers to God. I did not want others to know what I was asking God for. When I walked alone, was scared, or hungry, I prayed. I was always praying about something.

School was strict in the Caribbean. I remember we would get lashes when we were either late or unprepared. This was not by our parents but by the teachers or the headmistress. Even failing test or getting answers wrong would warrant hits across the fingers with a wooden ruler. There was one subject in math that for the life of me I could not understand. To make matters worse, I knew this teacher did not care for me. I had a test coming the next day, and I was *terrified*. All I could think about was getting beaten for failing that math test. That night after saying my prayers, I got into bed and stared at the ceiling, too nervous to sleep, thinking about the upcoming tests and what was sure to be the outcome.

During the night I had a dream about a lady teaching me a different way to do the math calculation that I was struggling with in school. Her method seemed long and complicated, but for some reason, the way the angel explained it I understood it. The rest of the night I rested well. I woke with a confidence I never experienced before. I jumped out of bed, said my prayers, showered, got dressed, and went to school. I must have smiled the whole way there. I could not wait to take the test. This teacher would not be beating me today.

As I walked in, the test was already written on the board. We were told not to talk to each other as we went to our seats. Instructions were to write the calculations at the side of the problems. She did not want just the answer; she wanted to see how we solved the problems. I glanced at the math and went to work. It was a pleasure for me. I answered every math problem, and next to it were my calculations. I mastered it and got every question right. Let me say that again, I got every question right.

Because my calculations were different from Ms. D, she called me to the front for me to give an explanation. Even though my calculations were all written next to the problems, I still had to explain to her my seemingly complicated process. Now she was the one who did not understand. I should have given her lashes (why didn't I think of that then). I explained it with such confidence it left her speechless. To me, her way was short and difficult. My way was long and easy.

After this, my relationship and faith in Jesus grew. When alone, I would talk with God more. I did most or all the talking. I knew that the Lord sent that angel to teach me the math. I was so grateful, and I knew, on God I could depend.

I started having more dreams, but some were more complicated. In time I started to understand them better. I dreamt often, and I learned to watch the events that would happen in my life. Some dreams are still so vivid in my memory. Many of them came to pass, but there is one dream that I still have not gotten the full meaning.

One of my sisters said I must be Joseph the Dreamer. They got tired of always hearing about my dreams. Initially, I did not think to ask the Lord what the dreams meant, but I learned. One night, I dreamt that there were so many big white sheets and a few small white garments hanging on the clothesline in the backyard. Everything was so white. I didn't know what this dream meant, and no one else seemed to know either. To my family it seems to be just another one of my dreams. A few days later, one of my aunts fell very ill. My mother took my sister and I to visit. While listening to their conversation and looking intently at my aunt, I realized that the big white sheets in the dream meant-sickness. The bigger the sheets, the greater the illness. From that time on, when I dreamt of white clothing, I knew that someone would get sick or was sick. The dreams did not scare me; they just prepared me for what was about to happen.

One morning I went next door and told my aunt about a dream I had. I said to her, "Last night I saw a small new wood house built in front of our house. It was small, made of new wood, and it leaned on one side. They (the carpenters) didn't do a good job." Suddenly, she panicked. She asked my older sister to take one of her sons to the doctor that morning. She apparently understood the dream more than I did at that time. The previous day my aunt's son had gone diving in water that was too shallow. He had cut his head. Even though this left a deep exposed wound, my aunt did not think it was serious enough to warrant a doctor's visit.

When my sister returned with my cousin, she gave the doctor's report. The doctor said the boy was lucky. If auntie had waited another day, it would have been bad for him because tetanus had started to set in. From then on, I watched my dreams and paid close attention to what came to pass. I enjoyed having dreams and visions, especially when they bought joy and prepared me ahead of time of what would happen. I didn't enjoy those dreams where someone would die, because I would be scared of them and wish I didn't get any more dreams.

I noticed that some of my scariest dreams were related to my father. He would have such angry and violent outburst, and I could tell before they happened. If I dreamt about rough seas with high crashing waves, I learned that this meant he would scream and terrorize the house in the morning. If I dreamt of blazing fires with the flames reaching tremendous heights, this meant that he would terrorize the house at night when he came home from work. Trouble, trouble, trouble! I could sense that something was about to happen.

My mother was so vulnerable to him. From a young age I felt the need to watch out for her. She could not or would not protect herself. I lived in constant fear of him hurting her. I knew if no one was watching, he would use that opportunity to strike. I've seen the fights and heard the arguments. More than one is one too many. He should have kept his hands to himself. She did not deserve to be choked, humiliated, and treated like nothing. Who deserves that?

I was too young to do anything. I wished I could protect her, but I lived in fear of him too. We would run next door to get help from her brother but even my uncle got tired of her always going back. I used to love my father so much, but the love turned to resentment—and possibly hatred. I remember so many sleepless nights as I waited for my dad to come into our room and *kill* us. He would often say that he would. I lost all respect for him. Such a bad dislike for him was growing inside of me. If he only knew what I thought of him, I wondered what would he have done to me?

My fears ate me up on the inside. I prayed, I cried out to God on our behalf. "Lord, help her, help us. Lord, send him away. Lord, take him so far away that he never comes back."

My dad used to show us his passport and tell us, "Look, I can go to any part of the world." Those old passports would have the world map on the inside of the covers. He would pick a place and tell us that he will go there. I always looked forward to the day when he would tell that he is leaving to go to some faraway part of the world. That day never came; he never kept that promise. We all eventually left him at home. His son, his wife, and all four daughters.

I believed my mother loved him too much to let him go or she was too scared of him that's why she didn't leave. Why stay? He's so rude and disrespectful to her and to us, his children. My mother believed in her marriage vows. Holy Matrimony. Her parents never wanted her to marry him. She already had two children, but they were hoping she would not marry him. They begged her not to marry him.

If you asked her anything about marriage, she would say, "My sister says when you get married, you have to stay with your husband." I don't care what her sister said. The sister's husband was never so stupid to raise his hand at her. It made me believe that my mother, though scared of her husband, wanted to stay with him. After the fights, when they made up, she would treat him like he was someone special. This angered my older siblings. I overheard them fussing about her. They wished that she didn't go back to him. They feared him, had no love for him, and wished he wasn't there. They couldn't wait until they were older to get away from home and far away from him. I wondered who would look out for mother when they were gone.

I started to doubt my prayers, thinking I must be praying wrong. Could it be that we were praying for my father to go and my mother was praying that he stays? Something was not working here. I started to blame God for what is happening. Secretly, I began to doubt God. Yes, I would pray, thanking Him for being with us, but felt that God wasn't helping me.

Every argument, every fight, I would tell God, "Daddy is bigger than Mother, but Lord, you are bigger than Daddy. Make him stop and listen." But I didn't get an answer. My fears were getting the best of me. I felt that man was going to kill her. He doesn't want her but doesn't want her to leave. He's always threatening to kill her. Can somebody do something? This is where I had a conflicted faith in God. I trusted that He was there for me, but I didn't understand why the situation remained the same. "Lord, I believe. Help thou my unbelief" (Mark 9:24).

I started to see my father as ***bad*** and ***strong***. I felt like he could do anything he wanted and get away with it. He was overpowering and threatening. How did he get to be like this. He was not like his dad. My grandfather was a man of God, honorable, respectful, caring and loving. He would come to speak with my dad about his wrong and disrespectful behavior and my father would shout and carry on with no respect.

I saw my mother as ***good*** and ***weak***. She was not perfect, but she cared and showed her love for us. She worked hard (on the plantation) to provide for us. The burden of providing for us fell on her.

# Help Me, Please

Daddy's priest would come by. My father respected him and spoke so highly of him, always boasting about the man's children. He constantly spoke so highly of them you would wonder if they were his. "What about us?" I would ask myself. He seems to show respect to his friends, their family, and those that he drank (alcohol) with. So often I wanted to tell the reverend what was happening in our home, but I was scared Daddy would beat the life out of me when he found out. What can I do? Where do I go from here?

When my father walked the street, people shouted out to him, the young children ran up to him, calling him godfather. He was godfather of so many kids. He joked and laughed with them, and if he had any money in his pocket, he would give them change to get ice cream, candy, or gum. They made him feel important. He made them feel important. At home, it was a different world. He did not treat or make his children feel important. He called us anything he liked, and what he said to us would burn us on the inside. *Stop.* Nothing hopeful, nothing inspirational. We at home had to beg him for anything we wanted. He would say, "Remind me again in an hour." We had to constantly go before him and ask for a quarter.

What an awful shame! How small and insecure it made us feel.

Once I saw my father beat my brother (fifteen) and my sister (eleven) without mercy. When he got to work the tea in his flask had churned. He could not wait to get home. He got in the yard, put down his work bag, and took out his anger and frustration out on them. Their screams penetrated my innermost being and I still remember as if it happened yesterday. It seemed the whole neighborhood heard their cries and screams. I was about five, but I vowed right there that I would never marry. *I said I would have my kids* by myself *and raise them* by myself. *That way, no man can hit them. What else was I a five-year-old-girl supposed to think? I knew I didn't want anyone who acted like my father in their lives.*

For years after that, when I looked at my father, all I saw was the monster in him. I hated to admit what I felt for him. That incident was a true nightmare. I cried so much and for such a long time over that incident. Nothing would take the pain away no matter how hard I tried.

At home they had a nickname for my father. I believed my mother gave it to him. *(She would refer to him as the devil).* My siblings knew who she meant every time she mentioned that name, and they would tense up. On the other hand, I hated that name. It scared me. It made me want to vomit. I didn't like it. That name was very distasteful, nasty, and derogatory. I never used it. It was so evil. If that is what he showed her, or that is how she saw him, why is she still with him?

As young as I was, I did not want to arouse his anger and for him to start cursing and scaring everyone. I just couldn't understand how I could love him so much when he is so mean and evil. I had so much inner conflict over him. A fear would run through me and gripped my stomach. I never knew what to expect from him, but I knew his attitude was so terrible that no one looked forward to him coming home from work.

There would be a deep sense of nervousness when he is approaching the house. I didn't have to see him or hear his voice, but I could always sense his presence when he is approaching, and I would announce to the others, "Daddy is coming." Then they would scatter. My mother and older sister told me that I would wake up, announce that he is coming, and go back to sleep. I was always 100 percent accurate. They said I never missed predicting his arrival, whether by car or walking. Once he reached within a certain distance from the house, I knew.

One day my mother came into the house and I followed her. She stood in the doorway looking outside and put her hands over the door frame. Next thing I saw was my father moving towards her in a lower position. No noise, no argument, in the quiet, he came behind, grabbed the wooden chair and swung it. I screamed out, 'Ma look'. Mother turned just in time to block the chair with her hand. Was he aiming for her neck or to strike her? It would have knocked her out of the door. Upon realizing what he did, he dropped the chair and ran.

She put her hand to her chest and cradled it with the other hand. She went outside to where the family was congregating and told them what happened. They called for a taxi to take her to the doctor. The doctor had them go to the police station to file the complaint and then go to the hospital. They kept her in the hospital, I don't recall for how long, but she had a cast from her shoulder to her wrist.

Because of this incident, the police came to take statements from any witness. The doctor sent her first to the police station to file charges against my father, and then to the hospital. Because her hand was broken and the incident reported, there would be a court case.

Two policemen came to the house to take statements from all who saw the incident. They spoke with my father first. I could not believe my ears at what he was saying. My father stood in my presence and boldly and blatantly lied. The police wrote every lie he said. I kept looking him in the face.

The police explained to me that because I had witnessed a crime, I had to give a statement. Then it was my time to speak. My father said to me, "Go ahead, tell them what I said is the truth." I stared at him in disbelief. I could not speak. The police looked at me and asked me again. My father was looking me straight in the face, telling me, "Go ahead, tell them what I said is the truth." I stared right back at him in disbelief. I was so scared of him I could not speak. The officers were speaking to me while my father was staring me in the face. My fear of him was getting the best of me, making me fidgety and uncomfortable.

I was thinking about what would happen to me when the police leave. One of the officers asked my father to leave the room so they could speak with me privately. My father was so angry at me. He shouted, "I know that you will tell them the truth. Go ahead and tell them". One of the officers took him out of the room and the other one stayed with me to ask questions about the incident.

The officer didn't have to ask me much of anything because I sang like a songbird. I could not hold it back and told them everything. My fear of my father grew. It was a scary, unhealthy relationship. I would be so scared to pass by him, and at night was worse. Instead of dreams, I started to have nightmares. The house was made with a partition that divided each room, but the partition did not reach the ceiling. I would dream that Daddy would come over the partition and kill me. Talk about torment. I would lay in bed very still and stare at the partition until I fell asleep.

I was eleven years old when my mother left the house. She left with a broken hand and a bruised and crushed ego. I cried so much for her, sorry to see her go but also relieved of the pressure I felt when she was at home with him. She was no longer at home where she could be abused, beaten, cursed or threatened. I thought of her and cried silently so no one would know.

I shuddered to think of what would have happened to my mother if I wasn't there. My desire to protect her had caused me to follow her into the house and watch her. Someone had to look out for her welfare. I had reached the point where I couldn't trust him around her. She didn't seem to feel the danger I felt for her life. I sensed it. I couldn't help myself. The feelings were real. Was I the only one who felt that way? Didn't the other children feel that something was wrong?

Once my mother was gone, my brother tried talking to my father. He was a police officer and wanted to explain what it felt like and how bad it looked. My father cursed and said he didn't have to listen to him. My brother declared he doesn't have to take this behavior anymore and will be moving out. He moved next door to my grandmother and uncle's house. Later my brother got married and moved to the city, enjoying his new wife and expecting a baby.

One Thursday evening as I was walking to the school bus-stand with a friend, I heard someone called out, "Puss" (the nickname the family called me). I saw my brother Carroll standing there. I dropped my school bag and ran to him, jumping up into his arms. We hugged and kissed. I told him how much the family missed him and to come home with me. He said he couldn't because he is off to play police football but tell the family he will come on Saturday when he is off from work.

It never happened; for that evening, as he was returning from police football on a motorbike, he got into an accident when an unlicensed driver failed to stop at the stop sign. At the hospital, he was given penicillin. The doctor, not knowing he was allergic, never checked and it flooded his lungs.

On Saturday morning, we got the news that he was in the hospital and wasn't doing good. My mother was crying and while rushing to go to the hospital, got another set of news that he had just died. My mother passed out. The shock of it was too much for her. She fell to the ground and was just spinning around in circles uncontrollably. She was spinning so fast I could not see her head and assumed that my father had killed her. That was terrifying. After the funeral, my mother had to be under the doctors' care. The pain was unbearable for her. She couldn't cry; she just held her stomach. My brother left a wife and a two-month-old baby daughter.

When my mother left home, there were three sisters. I thought things would get better, for there is no one to curse, beat, or threaten. But I was wrong. The cursing and the threatening continued. When he had something to say, he would open the doors and windows so that all the neighbors could hear him. He would go out on the steps and curse at the top of his lungs. Oh, how embarrassing. You could hear that man half a mile away.

Iola, the oldest of the three sisters, decided to leave home. She told no one. She went to work one day and didn't bother to come home. It broke my heart; for I needed her warmth, love, care, and to feel secure. What am I going to do now? The house felt so empty, but I had a greater emptiness inside that couldn't be filled. With my mother away; my brother's passing;

and now Iola, the older sister, gone, the house was not the same.

Without her I felt so lost and alone. I depended on her so much. I started to feel a numbness to the situation. The inner pain was too much to bear. When I needed that extra hug, the assurance that she gave me that all will be well, she was no longer there for me. She took over when Mother left, but it got too much for her, having to deal with Daddy and living under that type of stress, she decided to leave. She would meet me after school to see how I was doing. She was pregnant and happy. (My father used to say we are not bringing any grandchildren in his house.) She knew it was better to leave than to stay.

Next, it was the last two girls at home with Daddy. One would think that with a twelve-year-old and a fourteen-year-old, things would change and be better. Disturbing and arrogant as it was, the cursing and abusive behavior continued. I would look at that man and feel sorry for him. The slightest thing and he would let off some steam. "*Lord, have mercy,*" I prayed. "*Please help me to deal with this man.*" He would flare up early in the morning or late at night. It became habitual. We didn't know how or what to do to please him. What would we expect? Would he come home in a good mood? Or what was his day like?

Some cousins gave my father the nickname "Uncle Blowup". I don't know which one gave it to him, but it fit him perfectly. He found something to blowup about. Maybe he came to the point where he could no longer help himself, so he found some relief in blowing up.

One day I had to meet my dad at work. He gave me a package to bring home, but thinking I had time, I got off the bus and went by a friend. I didn't stay too long, maybe half an hour to one hour. On my way home, as soon as the house came into view, I got a nervous feeling in my stomach and instantly felt something was wrong. The closer I got to the house, the worse I felt. I had to practically drag myself home, so I decided to go the longest way. I said to myself, "If that man is home, he will not hit me."

When I reached the house, I saw a long tamarind rod all braided up that he had cut and planned to beat me with.

I said, *"Lord, this man is not going to hit me."*

My father asked, "Where were you?"

I looked him full in the face and lied. I said that I felt sick on the bus, so I got off and went by my friend and rested until I felt better. That was the end of that.

I slowly but surely got rid of that tamarind rod by cutting off pieces until it was gone.

# Off to High School

I attended a private high school on a partial government scholarship. It was not the school I'd prefer, but I had no say as to which school I wanted to attend. Daddy picked the school with the lowest tuition. The government granted a $25 scholarship per semester for five years, any more fees were the parents' responsibility. CHS was not one of the greatest, but it had one of the lowest fees. We had to provide our own textbooks, and it was so troublesome getting my father to buy my textbooks or the school supplies, which were important.

I felt so sorry for leaving the elementary school I was attending to go to this high school. I saw what my sister went through to collect the books from my father. If you remind him of the importance of the books, he would say, "Can't you borrow someone's books?"

"No, Daddy, they need their books to do their homework, and they're not going to lend me any." I did not get the books, so I could not study or do my homework. The teachers never tell you what lessons they were going to teach in advance. I wondered if I would have to go through what my sister went through. This made me regret getting a scholarship.

Getting the money to purchase the weekly pass for the bus was a dilemma. A few times I had to miss school, for there was no weekly pass. Lunch money was another issue. He would leave for work knowing there was no bread to make sandwiches or money for lunch, and when pressed for money, he would make us stay home. Once, he sent us to a family member who had nothing for himself. My father had a good job, got good pay, but taking care of us was not a priority.

After about two or three years in high school, the fee increased by $5. What a shock! What a horror! My father came home, saw the letter, and went off. He sent me to the liquor store. On my way, a friend (who lived about a half a mile away) heard his cursing and asked me what happened. I told her nothing really, just that the school fees went up five dollars. She stated he should be ashamed to carry on like that. He shouted, cursed, swore, and refused to pay the five dollars.

The school would read out the names of those who owed school fees and send them home. Every day he would send me to school, and they would send me home. Every day I complained. Every day he would send me back, and every day they would send me home. This went on for two weeks, back and forth. I refused to tell my mother what was going on. One day she came to visit me at the school around lunchtime and found out from one of my friends that I wasn't there, that I haven't been coming. She found out the reason and paid the five dollars.

My father decided to write the school a letter. He cursed the owner from her head to her toe, such derogatory and demeaning comments in the letter for over a $5 fee increase. I was so embarrassed. I didn't want to go to school anymore. I felt so ashamed, knowing what he did. I wondered how the teachers saw me, what they thought of me. I once asked him for twenty-five cents for a school notebook. That was on Friday. He said to remind him. All Saturday and Sunday, I reminded him because if I didn't, he would say, "You didn't remind me, so now you don't get any."

Monday morning, I was getting ready for school and my dad was getting ready for work, but I kept my eyes on him. I was making sure he didn't leave the house without giving me the quarter. I asked him again. He shouted that he doesn't have any damn money right now, then turned to leave the house. I turned away, not watching him anymore, but he came back in time to hear me say to my sister Edwardine, "He can't give me twenty-five cents for a book, but he can find money to buy liquor for his friends." *Oh boy!*

The look on her face scared me. She was trying to signal me that Daddy was back in the house. When I turned around, I was looking into two eyes that said, "Run for your life." I heard a small inner voice say, "Duck" (meaning lower your head). I missed his hand over my head by a second. He had swung a power slap at me, and I was just able to get out of his way. When I looked up, he said, "I was about to take your head off and put you in a corner."

The words he spoke, the look in his eyes, and his scary manner lasted all day. Usually, if I had something to say, I would make sure that he was not around. He knew that I would make some comment.

Daddy I need shoes. The soul of my shoes were worn out and whenever I passed the shoemaker I would asked him to fix it. (he was my mother's cousin and fixed it as best as he could. When the shoes could no longer be worn, I showed them to daddy and not having shoes to wear to school, he made me stay home for a week.

When I was seventeen years old, someone told my father that I was talking to a boy. I wasn't aware he knew. One night he caught the boy kissing me. Boy, oh, boy. I ran home and told my sister Edwardine, "Daddy saw me, and he is going to kill me. I mean, really kill me." By the time he got in the house, I had put on two pairs of pants and extra clothing to help protect against the lashes. He had no mercy as he let out his fury on me. I'm screaming the house down, and all that was in my mind is, *Daddy is going kill me.*

I didn't know what to expect as my screams penetrated the neighborhood.

Then the beating stopped, I sat on the bed crying, my back sore, hands and feet all wailed up, and body hurting all over. He came back inside, saying, "Where is she? Now I am going to kill her." Somehow his sister got between him and I, She tried to let me escape from him, but every time she said, "Run," he would take a swipe at me and I would jump behind her. They started arguing and wrestling over whatever was in his hand. She said again, "Run." Someone opened the door, and I dashed outside.

I was running for my life and going as fast as I can. Daddy was behind me, and my aunt was behind him. My cousins were shouting me on. "Run, run, run." Everyone was scared for me. I was desperate. My aunt caught up to him, and they started arguing again. That gave me some distance to getaway. I kept running and went to a friend's house, but she said, "This is the first place your father would come looking for you." Another friend was there and took me to a hiding place.

The next morning, with nowhere to go and Daddy off to work, I came home. Still scared, in pain, and nervous, I got some sleep and made sure to be out of the house by the time he came home. I was in the yard, not knowing what to expect, keeping an eye on him just in case he lunged at me. He didn't say a word but left the house after dinner. By the time he came home, I was asleep.

On Sunday, Daddy had a few friends over. Because I did not want to help with serving, I went outside and sat on a bench. My father was washing the rum glasses when one broke, cutting his hand. The bleeding would not stop, so his friends rushed him to the doctor. The doctor stitched and bandaged it, but the bandage was soaked in blood when he got home. His hand wouldn't stop bleeding. They were afraid and rush him back to the doctor. The doctor said it was because he was drinking alcohol and the hot temperature outside. The doctor changed his bandage and sent him home. I felt that he was being punished for what he did to me. In my anger, I said, "My father's hand should have been cut off." Edwardine told me that Daddy overheard what I said. I was so scared knowing he heard me. He said nothing to me about it.

My father never talked to us; all he did was cursed at us and belittle us as if we were not his. I knew I was wrong, but it wasn't worth his attempt to kill me. He forgot he made my mother pregnant with their first child at fourteen years. I know he did not want the same thing to happen to us. Every time he cursed; he would say that it runs in our mother's family. He would say, "Your grandmother got pregnant early, your mother got pregnant early, your sister got pregnant early, and it will happen to all of you."

He was the one who got mother pregnant early. By the time my mother was seventeen, she had two kids for him, one at fifteen and the other at seventeen years old. They got married soon after that. It was a marriage that her parents tried to discourage her from doing. They saw in him what she couldn't see. Against all the odds, she married him.

My last sister Edwardine left home to go and live with our mother in America. I was left at home with my 4 year-old nephew and my father. I wondered what would happen now. Nothing new, the same father, the same temperament, the same controlling frightful man. Nothing changed. I was expecting things to change. I was glad to have my nephew there with me. I could not imagine being alone in the house with my dad. The emptiness and fear of my father was too much.

My father cried so much when Edwardine left. His conscience got the better of him. He had cursed her about a week before. My mother must have gotten wind of it all the way across the seas and sent for her. My father acted in disbelief but had too much pride to apologize. How embarrassing, the things he said. Knowing this, I expected him to change.

It came to the point that I was operating on raw nerves. I told the Lord, "Please don't let me have a nervous breakdown. They like to call you crazy once you go to the mental hospital." I was so shattered and broken on the inside. No one should have to deal with all that nonsense. I was so emotionally drained and close to the breaking point. I just could not take it anymore. I felt there was no one to talk with. It seems no one understood. Trying to hold it all together had reach its breaking point.

One day I asked a cousin (Jen) to go to the doctor with me. I had $20. I paid for our bus fare to the doctor and back. I paid the doctor's fee and the balance of the money paid for the medication. The doctor asked me what was wrong.

I said, "Doctor, I feel like a clock that's been wound too tight, and the spring is broken." He said, "Tell me a little about your situation." I was shaking so much, he gave me time before I could talk to him.

He prescribed four different meds for me to be taken at different intervals. Two of them finished in two weeks, one finished in three weeks, and the last one lasted for four weeks.

I don't remember much of what was going on at home while I was on the meds, for they kept me calm and at peace, and I was able to ignore whatever was happening around me. I knew that Daddy continued to act the same, but I could block him out and totally ignore him. I had such peace on the inside. The day I took the last tablet, I started to panic and wondered what I would do now. Oh no, I wanted to go back to the doctor, but I had no money.

That night things just exploded. I had started a business course at an institute doing typing and other skills to help me get a job. I sat at the table, practicing my typing when I remembered that Iola was coming the next day to help me with the laundry and asked me to soak the linens overnight. I went outside, filled the tub with water and some detergent, put the linens in, and came back inside. I'd just started back typing when my father came out of his room, cursing at me, saying that I was home all day, and now at night, I was washing.

I just stared at him. I wanted to explain that Iola was coming the next day to do the laundry and asked me to soak the linens overnight. He was cursing, so I just stared at him and said nothing. The next minute he pulled out a chair from the table to swing at me. When he brought the chair to his shoulder, I kept staring at him and didn't move or shift. (It was the same situation with my mother). I was so broken and weak, I felt whatever he wants to do, just let him do it. I could not run, could not move, could not hide, could not scream..

He shouted, "So you're not scared of me. You're not moving." I just continued to stare him in the face. He put the chair down, continued cursing at me, then went back to his room. I said, *"Lord, I can't take this anymore, and I refuse to live like this."*

I asked my cousin to call my sister Iola and tell her to come and get me. Iola sent back a message that she will get me in the morning. Half an hour later, I hear the familiar sound of her husband's motorbike. That was a God send. My brother-in-law said, "I don't want trouble with that man, so I think we should go to the police station.

I really didn't want to go to the police, but I knew I couldn't live in that situation anymore. "Okay," I said, got on his bike, and off we went to the police station to file a claim, stating that I wanted to move out and didn't want any trouble. They sent two officers.

They knocked on the door. I was hiding behind the officers. My father got up from sleeping and answered the door. When he saw the officers, he got a little nervous.

They said, "It is your daughter." He asked, "Is she all right? Did something happen to her?"

They said, "She's okay. She wants to leave and asked for our protection that nothing happens to her."

He sat down, and the officers sat next to him, one on each side. The officers said to me, "Miss, you can come in and get your clothes." The few things I had, I put them in a bag. I gave my father the keys and left.

I was in total shock. Still couldn't believe what had happened. I knew that I couldn't stay there anymore. My nerves were at the breaking point. I was losing control. I stayed with my sister, and she nurtured me. Just being in her presence, just being able to talk with her was like therapy. She poured love into me like when I was young. I needed her. I thanked God it happened without any violence. I thank God that I had a place to stay. She knew quite well what our father was like.

I cried so much. I needed to get the pain out, get rid of all that hurt and nervousness. It was a relief. I didn't mean for it to end this way, but I had no choice. He was a man full of pride. One of my sisters used to say, "Daddy knew half of the population, and the other half knew him." He kept company with those in authority. I wondered how his friends saw him. Do they really know him for who he is, or is it because they didn't have to live with him, it didn't matter?

My stay with Iola lasted one month. When my mother got word that I had left home, she panicked. Mother was living in New York, far out of my father's reach and sight. The news she received said that I had run away from home, and no one knew where I was. I now had a home where I felt comfortable and at peace, where I could go places and feel a sense of freedom. I got my resume ready and started looking for a job, the taste of life.

# The Siblings

This union produced five children. First, a girl (Eugene), then a boy (Carroll), then three girls (Iola, Edwardine, and I). I used to compare life to theirs, always commenting that Eugene had it so much better. She lived next door with my grandma (Mother B) and didn't have to put up with Daddy. Because we lived so close Eugene came over, except when Daddy was around.

My oldest sister, Eugene, was twelve years older than me. She never had any tolerance for Daddy. I was six years old when she left for London. Eugene would always tell us about our grandpa (my mother's dad). Once Eugene got word of Daddy's abuse of Mother, she said it wasn't like that when she was around. She felt such furor and bitterness toward him.

My older brother Carrol was my true love. His nickname was Smutt. I think he was everyone's love. The family loved him and looked up to him (except my father). Daddy never showed him any love and made his life difficult. Carrol never let that stop him. My eldest sister and my brother were the first two grandchildren for my father's parents. We used to say they had the best of both worlds.

My brother looked out for us and showed us how to make and fly kites, pitch marbles, roll the wheel, climb trees, and put me on his back, helping us do whatever we wanted. He was the sweetest brother anyone could have. I loved him so much. When I was in elementary school, I participated in sports. At the stadium, among my schoolmates and teachers, I heard someone called, "Puss" (one of the names they called me). I hopped over those benches and jumped into his arms. Oh, I felt like a true princess. That's the way he always made me feel. We hugged and kissed and laughed with each other. He was in the police training program at that time, so we didn't see him often.

When I returned to my seat, the teachers and students started calling me Puss. They kept teasing me and would not stop. When I got home, I told my mother to tell him not to call me Puss anymore, but he never stopped.

He died at the young age of twenty-two years. It was ten days after my twelfth birthday. His death sent shockwaves through the whole family, through the neighborhood, through his friends. His life touched many and left a true impression on everyone. When he died, he took a part of me with him. The pain wouldn't go away. Experiencing such pain so early, nothing in my later years could hurt as much. His death had created a numbness where I couldn't allow myself to feel the pain of others.

I remembered looking in the casket and begging him to get up. "Please get up. Can you hear me? You look so good. There is nothing wrong with you. Don't let them keep you in there. Please get up, get out, please, please." His departure left me helpless and empty. When you lose someone that close to you, it blows your mind. You can't seem to understand or let go of what happened.

My second sister, Iola, was a real treasure. She is six years older than me and she tried her best to take care of us when mother left. The cooking, washing, cleaning, shopping all seemed to fall on her. It was as if she was always working. Once I had a bad migraine, and before I could get out of bed, I had vomited all over myself and the bed. She came in, cleaned me, put me in a chair, stripped the bed, put on fresh linens, mopped the floor, and went back to doing the laundry. We had no running water or washing machine, you went to the pipe with a bucket to fetch water. I always remember how much she loved and took care of me.

I suffered from migraines early on but didn't know the name of the illness and never went to the doctor. I would tell them I have dark spots in my eyes. I would look at someone and see only half of their face. I could not understand what was happening, but I knew that I would be sick. These headaches came with nausea and vomiting and were such a scary experience.

My third sister, Edwardine, was almost two years older than I. With just the two of us at home, we had to learn how to be there for each other. Living with Daddy became impossible. Trying to please Daddy was a job in itself.

I don't know how growing up at home with Daddy affected the others, but it sure took its toll on me. I was so close to having a nervous breakdown. It is only so much one can take. Maybe I'm not as strong as the others. I seem to live in the past, not letting go enough to move forward, in order to hold on to the present. That negativity followed me throughout my life, with me always bringing up the past and referencing something Daddy did or said. I sometimes blamed myself for not doing anything. What could I have done?

I remember running to get my uncle to come and help. He would put Daddy in a headlock causing him to release my mother. A few days later she would be back with him. This became so tiring. One night my uncle was asleep, and I was screaming and knocking at his bedroom window that Daddy was choking my mother and was going to kill her. He jumped out of bed and rushed over. He put a chokehold on Daddy, causing him to release his sister. He took my mother home with him. Not having enough clothes on and the night chill, he caught a bad cough and got ill. He became so tired and worn-out with the situation and said, "Don't call me anymore. If that is how she wants to live her life, it is her business."

My grandmother had taken as much as she could. She didn't speak to my father, and with his stinking attitude, he didn't seem to care. When my mother came from the hospital, she lived next door with her mother, her brother and his family. That was too close for comfort. After all, we shared the same driveway and the same backyard. I felt she could not be safe living so close. I longed for her to move far away. She stayed and took care of her mother, who was ill. I don't know if it was love; I think she feared him. I can't understand the logic.

The memories of my father and mother were a constant nightmare, with me screaming in my mind for him to stop and for mother to get a good hold of something to knock him out.

Eugene, Iola, and Edwardine seem to have shaken off the past and made a good life. I carried it with me wherever I went. I couldn't let go. Maybe I saw more than they did. When I was young I remember always asking to sleep in my parents room. I felt I needed to put some distance between the two of them (for me, it was a way of protecting her). I saw in my father something that no one else seemed to have noticed. I saw his lack of love and respect for his family, his ignorance, his wickedness, his disrespect.

I saw her weakness and vulnerability. Home with Daddy was a living nightmare. We went nowhere, and every time you asked him, he would say *no*. I find myself staring at him and trying to figure him out.

Not knowing much better, I blamed God for everything. I prayed so hard for a change in the home. Send him away Lord. Make him stop. Nothing happened.

# The Painful Years

Carroll (my brother) moved away from home in 1966.
He died in March 1967.
My mother moved out in 1966 with a broken hand.
My sister Iola moved away from home in 1967.
My paternal grandfather died in 1968.
My maternal grandmother died in 1969.
My mother moved to America in 1971.
My sister Edwardine moved to America in 1972.
I moved out from home in 1973 to my sister Iola's home. One month later, I joined my mother.
My father died in 2005 at the age of eighty-three.
My mother died in 2007, two weeks before her eightieth birthday.
My father called me *Sputnik*, my mother called me *Elly*, my grandmother called me *Juggy*, my siblings called me *Puss*. These nicknames were given to me when I was a baby, everyone called me by the character they loved. No one called me by my real name (given by Daddy) because no one liked it.

# Welcome to America

Coming to America was unexpected and something I was unprepared for. Everything happened so fast, and I was totally unprepared. While still living at home with Daddy, I got my passport. I was enjoying the peace and tranquility at my sister's home while looking for a job. I treasured living there with her and her family. I was just getting used to living in such a peaceful environment, no noise, no fear, everything so peaceful and relaxing when I got a Visa for America.

Coming to America, I had no idea what to expect. My mother took me to her job because she didn't want me to be in the house alone. Then she got me a job doing housework. I said, "Not me, I am not doing it." Well, she won this fight. She got me a babysitting job that was far away. I couldn't stay with the family and only came home on weekends. I just couldn't handle it. I would either quit or get fired. None of the jobs lasted more than two weeks. I wasn't ready for that work, and it sure wasn't ready for me.

My mother said, "If you don't work, you still have to pay rent." I couldn't believe my ears. She said since I didn't want to work, I would have to pay rent. She divided the rent, phone, electric, and gas bill and told me what I owed. Since I was looking for a job and calling all the agencies, I ran up the phone bill. When the bill came, she said this is twice the amount they usually pay per month and give me half of the bill. Complaining didn't solve the problem. I had to borrow money from my sister. I found a job soon after.

My mother and I once got into an argument. She said. "I am sending you back home." I said, "good, for that is where I want to go."

She looked at me and said nothing. I should have kept quiet. She never gave me back my passport, and I was stuck. Sometimes, I would wonder if I was expecting too much from my mother. I wanted more for my mother. I felt she deserved better and so much more. She was the only daughter for her dad, and he treated her like a princess. I just didn't understand. I thought that we would be close to building back the relationship we had. I was looking to fill the void that was created when she left home.

I had that need of wanting to protect her, still worrying about her. One day I asked her why she stayed with him. She just stared at me in disbelief and kept silent. That was so disrespectful of me. I figured I had gotten burned so badly by that relationship, I couldn't hold back any longer. I needed for her to conversate with me and share her feelings. For so long

I carried the responsibility for her safety, and I needed some answers. She later said she stayed to be there for us, to protect us.

I told her no, that is not so. Don't ever tell me that. I told her not to put that guilt or responsibility on me. I reminded her of the time he beat the children so bad and she did nothing. If you could not protect yourself and you could not protect your children, the best thing was for you to make plans to leave and go far, then once you make a life for yourself, you can get your children. Being home you could not help us or yourself against his fury. We were more scared for your life and safety than for him abusing us.

# Part 2

---

## My Spiritual Father: Jehovah God
## My Relationship with God

I don't remember at what age I gave my life to Jesus Christ. Accepting Jesus Christ as my Savior and Lord was easy. I believed in Him, so I wanted to serve Him. Living the life of a true Christian was not as easy as I thought. I assumed that I would be changed and walking in faith and in righteousness. I was not prepared for the challenges nor did I realize the things I had to give up. I accepted the Lord, but I continued to live the way I was accustomed to living. I always loved dancing, and no one could get me to give up the partying. When anyone would tell me about my drinking, I would quote the text, "Drink no longer water but a little wine for thy stomach sake" *(1 Tim. 5:23)*. They would ask me what's the matter with my stomach.

The problem I had in being a Christian was I bought all my baggage with me. All the bitterness, anger, resentment, unforgiveness, abuse, brokenness, low self-esteem, hatred— everything that I should have left behind and done away with, I held onto. My unforgiveness got in the way of my relationship with the Lord. My conversations centered around my father. I needed to forgive, to let go, to walk away from all the pain, and to not look back. I once saw myself in a dream carrying loads of luggage. I would get tired, stop, put down my luggage. When I got ready to go, I would pick them up again. I never realized it was all the garbage of pain and hurt I was taking with me everywhere I went.

One of my downfalls was the death of my brother. I could not let go. I constantly asked God why. Also, my mother's abuse at the hands of my father, praying that she would leave him and be safe.

I attended an Anglican church, and I was about eleven or twelve years old when I got confirmed (confirmation). I always said when I leave my dad's house, I will not go to an Anglican church anymore. My decision was based on how my father lived, always the friendly and polite person in church and with his friends but was a monster at home—two completely different personalities.

I can remember my dreams and visions. I would get a dream or vision almost every night, and when I awoke and realized I did not have a dream or vision, I would be worried.

"Lord," I asked, "what happened? Did I do or say something wrong? How come You didn't give me a dream or vision last night?" The dreams and visions made me feel special and chosen, and always gave me a heads-up on what would happen, preparing me for the following days' events.

I had just started a new job when I dreamt about a big yellow snake that had wrapped its body around the office and wore a crown on its head. "Lord, who is this person?" I asked. I was not good at interpreting dreams, but I was learning fast. As I entered the office, the person was waiting for me. She assumed because I was new to the company, she could take advantage. She was in control, or so she thought. I said, "Good morning," and put my bag on the desk. She made some comments about my work. I turned around and instantly saw the face of the snake on her.

The manager had spoken to her about my work production. He had no idea what was going on, but after that confrontation, the manager brought us into his office. I explained that I started with a two weeks' worth of work backlog the other person had left behind, plus the daily work that came in, and everyone wants their work done right away. One manager had the nerve to put stickers on the work pile:

First pile said, "Do now."

Second pile said, "Priority."

Third pile said, "Do first thing."

The Lord had given me that job, and I was grateful for the pay increase. Initially, the job was difficult, but I liked the pay. I prayed and asked the Lord to show me how to do the job and *He did*. I would pray on my way to work, when I got there, and when I got home. After this incident, apologies were exchanged. My dream of the snake was so accurate.

One night I had a dream about someone on the job. I did not quite understand the dream, but in it, the Lord showed me someone and warned me to stay away from that person. The next day a coworker accused me of an incident that I knew of but did not inform her. My friend Dee was there and said nothing. I asked Dee to tell Kate the truth (since she was present) and explain what really happened, but Dee kept quiet.

Dee put her hand on my shoulder and said, "Don't worry, I am your friend, I have your back." I moved her hand off my shoulder and said, "Last night, I had a dream, and in it, God told me you were not my friend and to stay away from you." Dee was so embarrassed and ashamed. I found out later that Dee caused the confusion and then acted as if she knew nothing. I would often tell them the Lord would show me things before it happened. After this incident, we kept our distance.

Dreams, visions, talks, laughter, being in his presence, whatever it was—being in God's presence made me feel good. I felt His strength, His love, His joy, and the fullness of His presence. I enjoyed our many conversations anywhere, anytime, all the time. *I was so in love with Him. Not just love Him or like Him; I was in love. He is my joy, my peace, my rock, and my happiness. I felt so much love when He calls my name or when He speaks to me. Everything about Him had me on cloud nine.* Imagine the Lord calling you. You feel so important. I was the happiest I can recall. Nothing and no one had ever made me feel that good. I walked on air and was happy and excited.

I don't know how to better describe my feelings. When you are in His presence, you feel His love all around you. You could be in a room with one hundred or one thousand people, and the Lord singles you out.

The Lord chose you to reveal His attention. The Lord says, "to draw near to Him, and He will draw near to you" *(James 4:8)*. I drew near and nearer to Him. God said to come up higher. I felt as I was taking a ladder to reach Him. I finally reached Him; and His Presence was overwhelming, so light, so powerful, something to desire, to want. His wisdom, knowledge, and understanding are being poured into you. You feel as if his presence lifted you and made you a different person.

Ask anyone who has been in the presence of the Lord. Nothing on earth can compare to it. You want to stay in God's presence if possible. You do not desire any earthly things, for you know they cannot compare to what you have experienced. I used to tell my close friend how much I want her to experience the presence of the Lord or have a visitation because you will not be the same. Just hunger for the Lord, just set aside everything and wait on Him. I would say, "You have to experience His fullness, His joy, His peace, His presence." To experience His anointing, you feel as if you are in love. You must desire His presence. You must want it that much that you would be willing to give up everything to have it.

I walk in super confidence, super joy, knowing without a doubt that I was in the presence of the Lord.

The happiness and love you encounter make it a joy. Your laughter sounds different; you smile so much. I used to get teased about what I was thinking about. My friends would ask if I was thinking about a boyfriend. I was so happy, and it showed. When I praise the Lord, it seems to be forever. I did not want to stop praising the Lord. Lord, I want to...

- talk with You like **Adam**

- walk with You like **Moses**

- believe in You like **Abraham**

- trust You like **Joshua**

- praise You like **Daniel**

- dance for You like **David**

- wait on You like **Joseph**

- please You Like **Josiah**

Many times during praise and worship, I would be dancing and felt like someone was dancing with me. I would have one hand in the air as I was being twirled around. Sometimes I would be in deep conversation with the Lord and would fail to see other persons listening and watching. I would continue talking and laughing with God. My family would stare at me as if I were crazy. No, I am not crazy, and I would not stop the laughter or the conversation. Those moments were too precious to stop. I was not ashamed. I pray that others would someday experience a loving relationship and deep faith in the Lord. They would desire more of his wonderful presence.

God loves us so much. Think about His love for humankind. Be grateful to Him and tell Him how much you appreciate Him. The more time you spent in His presence, in prayer, in meditation, in His waiting room (being still before Him) and reading His Word, the stronger you became, and you are drawn closer to Him. You learn to hear His voice, to feel His presence for greater discernment. Your life changes for the better. Your passion, peace, purpose, and power greatly increase.

You start to cherish those alone moments when you are with Him. They become so precious, beautiful quiet times to talk, laugh, sing, dance, pray, walk, embrace the joy, smell the flowers and His sweet aroma. Embrace His wonderful presence and be at peace. Nothing brought me greater fulfillment than to be in the presence of the Lord. I learned to be still before Him, to wait on Him, to enjoy his presence. God appears in the stillness.

# The Waiting Room

I would lie in bed and imagine being in the doctor's office and having to sit in the waiting area until a room was prepared for me, then the assistant would take me to my room. I would lie there so still (keeping my mind clear of all distractions), waiting on the physician/God to enter. I always knew that the Physician was in the room as soon as He touched me. He (God/Physician) would always work on my head, never on the body. I never saw Him but only felt His touch. His team would be around the bed, dressed in white with the necessary equipment in hand.

Every assistant carried a specific piece of equipment, and God would reach out to the person that held what He needed. No talking was done. Each one knew the order, and when finished, the Physician would leave, followed by his team. This happened every time I went into His waiting room to be worked on. When finished, I would prayer and praise. I delighted in waiting and being worked on by Him.

Just being in His presence, lying there as still as I could, no thinking, just keeping my mind quiet. As soon as a thought entered my mind, I would erase it. It was my mind that I needed to be still, not the body.

That took some practice, but once you can quiet the mind, you are in control and be in a place where you could feel and observe the presence of the Lord.

It was through this "term" in God's waiting room that I developed a closer relationship with the Lord. I was in a place in the Lord where I felt I could talk to Him and could hear Him so often without distraction. No misunderstanding here. I would get dreams and visions so often that I became dependent on Him talking to me. My trust in Him was so elevated that I felt as if I was in a drunken stupor.

A friend once asked me why the Lord would always call on me and not on her. "What are you doing so differently?" I told her I spend much time in His presence praying. Being separated from family or friends did not affect me. I know who my God is. I know who I serve. I know who I was walking and talking with. I know who loves me and who I love. I know who protects me and cares for me. I know who I can depend on. It was as if all fear was gone.

I became super confident—to have that kind of relationship with the Lord; to live for Him and in Him, to love Him with all my heart, to put Him first; to hear and know His voice; to answer "Yes, Lord" to His will and His way; to know who I belonged to; to walk with, be in love, and be a part of Him, feeling so protected (going from the pit to the palace), experiencing royalty in its true purpose, being a bold witness for Him; to honor Him; to grow closer and closer every day, having a deeper understanding of who I am and whose I am. I walked feeling tall and proud. No one could tell me anything. I knew who my Father (God) is.

Once I had a confrontation on the job with a coworker. I looked the person in the face and asked him, "Do you know who I am? I am a child of God. God spoke to me this morning. When did He speak to you?" That was my defense. I felt so full of God (or myself), and I did not have anything else to say. The person became quiet, not knowing what to say. Using my faith to defend myself, I walked away feeling good as if I had won the battle.

# Daddy's Visit to New York

Many years later, my father came to New York to visit Edwardine and her family. On one visit, my mother kept insisting that I talk with him and forgive him. She would make me feel so guilty and say, "If your father should die and you didn't forgive him, you will be truly sorry." That was very hard for me to do, so on one of his visits I asked the pastor's wife (First Lady Hill) to be in the room with us, and she agreed.

The three of us were in the bedroom, and Lady Hill asked my father if he was okay with her being there since I needed her presence.

Daddy said politely, "Oh, my daughter, she made one mistake."

That was all it took. I immediately jumped off the dressing table I was sitting on. Luckily, Lady Hill was standing between my father and me. I repeated his statement. "I made one mistake, I made one mistake! You mean the night I brought the police for you." How dare this man say that. I couldn't control my rage. I told him how he treated us, how he would curse at us every day, morning, noon, and night. It was a constant nightmare. I reminded him how he never had anything good to say to us. He would tell us he didn't care and whatever he said he meant. How much he threatened us to beat us up, to harm and disable us, to even kill us. Who would want to live like that? How much can a person take? How low he made us feel. He treated us like we weren't his children. We lived under so much fear and pressure from him.

My father started crying uncontrollably, asking me to please forgive him, please, please, please. He said, "I am so sorry for what I did. Please, can you forgive me?" I said you told us that you are not sorry and whatever you said to us you meant it. You didn't care and that is what you showed us. He repeated his apologies and said he was truly sorry and if I could forgive him.

I stopped talking and with tears in my eyes said, "Yes, I forgive you."

Did I really mean it, for so much hurt and bitterness was still a big part of me? The next moment he was holding me.

While I was reminding my father for his bad treatment of us, I saw myself vomiting. I didn't vomit, but while I was releasing all that furry, it became too much for me and I closed my eyes. When I said I forgave him, the vomit seemed to stop flowing and some went back down my throat. I knew that he had stopped me before I got it all out. I needed to get it out, for there was too much pain left inside.

I wished I could get all the hurt, pain, resentment, unforgiveness, suffering, anger, bitterness, and distaste from in me. I didn't expect the conversation to go the way it did. I expected some disagreement and arguments. We never could say a word once he started talking to us, so I felt that he would have a lot to say.

Lady Hill said she was sorry I had to go through all that pain. She had no idea what was about to happen. All I told her is that my father was leaving for Barbados tomorrow and I needed to talk with him before he leave but because of his temper, I needed her there for support. I felt a little relief, but I was still hurting. He left an open wound that would take a lot of healing and care. He had taken my life away, destroyed my hopes, my dreams, destroyed my childhood and left me broken.

# Haughtiness and Pride

A friend was at my home, and before they left, they offered to pray. We joined hands, and they prayed for me and asked the Lord to remove the spirit of haughtiness. I did not receive it and asked myself why did she prayer like that. I assume she was not referring to me. Later in a conversation, she told me that the Lord had spoken to her about her own haughtiness and she repented.

At church, the pastor preached on haughtiness. In my arrogance, I said, "I know she's not speaking to me." On my way home, I stopped by a church where a pastor's friend was a guest speaker. I got there just to hear the end of his message, and the subject was *haughtiness*. I said, "Lord, I believe You are speaking to me." I repented. That message took the wind out of my sails. When I left the church, I was in a downward spin. I stopped at the corner store, got two wine coolers, and hurried upstairs. Once inside I drank one quickly and sipped the other. I had to look at my life, so full of faith but doing everything wrong (not in the order of God's will).

I had become so full of myself. "Lord," I asked, "what am I doing wrong? I do not have a house, car, or money in the bank. But I do boast in my faith in You." The Lord reminded me that those people I snub my nose at, He can save and deliver them from their situation and bring them out as He did for me. It was a wake-up call. It hit hard. I was torn up on the inside. I confessed my faults and repented for my sins. *Too much pride.* I had to think about my situation.

I did not realize I could be walking in faith, loving the Lord, and yet be living contrary to what the Lord wants. Pride is sin; haughtiness is sin. The Bible says, *"Pride goth before destruction and a haughty spirit before a fall" (Prov. 16:18).* My father used to say, "Too far east is west, and too far west is off the map." I wondered where I was in this situation.

I was not humble. I was not representing God the way He wanted me to. I was not setting a good example of love and forgiveness. When someone hurt me, I was not turning the other cheek, wasn't showing them love, and wasn't telling them about the love of God. I felt that God would fight my battles and protect and cover me, but that was not how God wanted me to handle the situation. We must walk in love and forgiveness. I asked the Lord to teach me to be humble. "Lord, teach me to walk in love."

*"Heal me O Lord, and I shall be healed; save me, and I shall be saved: for thou art my praise" (Jer. 7:14).*

I had a lot to learn, had much growing up to do. Walking in faith is one thing but walking in love is greater. *"And now these three remain faith, hope, and love. But the greatest of these is love" (1 Cor. 13:13).* I was broken and torn on the inside. I had to throw out everything and start at the beginning. If I thought I knew everything, I realized I knew nothing. I had to be taught. I cried, prayed, fasted, sulked and pitied myself. I learned it took more than faith to please the Lord.

"Change me, Lord," I cried. "I want to please you."

*"Create in me a clean heart. O God; and renew a right spirit within me" (Ps. 51:10).*

I meditated on the scripture day and night, for weeks, months, maybe years. "Lord, please help me," I cried. "I want to do your will. I want to walk in total obedience to You."

I thought I had lost it. God stripped me early, and it was good. I had to learn, heal, and grow. It was a great and valuable lesson that kept me in check.

I have seen some ministers doing things their own way and act as though no one can say anything to them (even if it is for their own good). They become so stiff or high-minded thinking they do not have to answer to anyone. They do not realize that people are watching them and thinking that if the minister is not upright, they too can do the same thing. Their congregation is watching, so are their loved ones, coworkers, family, relatives, friends, neighbors, and associates.

Sometimes people leave the church all burnt out and bitter, feeling deceived and betrayed. They call it *church hurt*, and some lose faith in God for what happened to them. I also was a victim of *church hurt*. Often, when people would leave the church, they blame the minister for what they experience. I always say you can tell me you love me all you want but you cannot show me if it's not there. Show me your love through your actions, and you will not have to say a word.

We read of David and Bathsheba and the sin they committed, and we read in *Psalm 51* how David cried out and repented before the Lord. No matter how big or how small, we must be humble and repent.

I was attending this church when the Lord told me it was time to leave. I did not know how to approach the pastor with my good news, so I asked the Lord if He could tell the pastor that He had called me to be somewhere else. One Sunday, during service, the pastor looked at me and asked, "Sister, are you planning to leave?" I said yes. He said he needed to speak with me after service. The pastor asked me not to go. I told the pastor the Lord said it was time for me to leave. The pastor would not receive it. I felt stuck.

It happened when I would go to church, the closer I got to the building, I would get sick. When service was over, I would run, and the further away I got, the better I felt. I made up my mind to leave. I could not understand the pastor. He knew the Lord wanted me to leave, yet he tried to stop me. Who does the pastor think is in control?

A friend of mine had recently opened a church, and I decided that is where I'll go. An elderly pastor opened a church and invited me. Without asking the Lord where He wanted me to go, I decided to join my friend's church. Not so, says the Lord. For the first time in my life I had an unexplained experience. I would get ready for one church, but I felt God's hand on my forehead leading me straight to the church He wanted me to attend. The elderly pastor was experienced, knowledgeable, and a great teacher. No slackness there. I learned fast. I grew in the things of God and quickly surrendered myself to Him.

The church had its own rules and by-laws. My complaint was that God had enough rules, commandments, and laws to live by and that should be our focus. Instead, we had to learn more rules. It was a boot camp. It was good training for the soul and spirit, but since it was not the church of my choice's, I always found something to fuss about.

I began to spend more time in my prayer closet and reading the Word. "Lord," I would say, "teach me how to praise you." I spent more time in His presence and His Word. Later the pastor asked me to lead the weekly prayer meeting. I fussed about that. I told her I do not know how to do it. Some people in the church can pray better than I can, why don't you ask them? I call the names of the people I felt could do a better job. She said nothing to me and that was the end of our conversation, or so I thought.

The prophet came to visit, and I told him I did not want to do it because they there are others who can do a better job than I can. The prophet said to me, "Girl, you'd better do what the Lord has called you to do." I said, "I didn't know the Lord had called me. Okay, I will do it." I asked the Lord to teach me how to pray. Soon, resentment followed by those who wanted the position. My response was, it was the Lord's decision and if they disagreed, they should speak to the Lord. I did not ask for the position, and I was quite happy praying in my closet, just me and the Lord. Later the pastor called me in the office and said, "You have no idea how much attitude I got for giving you the position others wanted."

It is in the closet that God nurtured and developed me. "Lord, teach me how to praise You. Teach me how to love and worship You. Lord, I want to please you in Spirit and truth." The more time I spent in the presence of the Lord, the closer I felt to Him, and the more I love Him. I felt so close to Him that whatever I said, I believe He heard me. I began to talk to the Lord as I would to a friend. I felt the Lord was ever so close, and I was breathing in His presence. I felt as if I had an invisible friend, someone who was always with me, could see me, speak with me. The only difference is that I could not see the person.

I felt so loved and smothered when the Lord called my name. I would say, "Call my name again, Lord, please call my name again." When the Lord would speak directly to me, I would tell Him how much I love hearing His voice. I told my friend Kerri that when she gets to know the Lord intimately, she will not ever want to go back. Having that bond and so much love between them, the things she valued before would not seem to hold that much value. Your value changes. You will desire to be in His presence above and before everything. If you think you are in love now, when you truly experience being in love with Him, you realize there's no comparison. Imagine loving someone so much, so wonderful, so powerful, you feel as if you can fly you are up in the heavens.

The Lord is my focus. He is my joy. When the Lord says, "Come back to your first love," He is saying to you that He created you and there was no one else. He is your first love, true love, eternal love, everlasting love, and your forever love. That is so powerful. You must be in the place of receiving to understand the power of God's love fully.

God's love for us is deep and strong. God is totally committed to us. Imagine Christ going to the cross for us. It was not an easy task (*Matt. 26:39*). And He (Jesus) went a little further and fell on His face and prayed, saying. *"Oh my Father, if it be possible, let this cup pass from me, nevertheless not as I will, but as thou will."* Jesus endured the pain and suffered the shame for us. Just think about it. What would make Jesus go to the cross for you? Who else would go to the cross to save us? Ask yourself who would you give up your life for.

I would tell the Lord I want to love Him more, I wanted to come up higher. In my love for Him I felt as if I was climbing a ladder without steps. I was at the bottom of the ladder looking up and some Supernatural force just carried me up higher. *The Lord said to focus on His love for us for His love is greater.* I focused on His Love and appreciated Him more.

Just think about the things God delivered you from. You are stranded far from home, feeling scared and alone, you call on the Father; and immediately, you feel a warm presence and suddenly you are not afraid anymore. You are at home, scared and alone, the Lord tells you to *anoint* yourself and the doors and windows. You meditate on the passage of scripture, *"The angel of the Lord encamps around those who fear Him and delivers them from all their fears" (Ps. 34:7).*

At home I am not afraid. I know without a doubt God is with me and His angels truly encamp around me. I am in a place of deep appreciation and gratitude for God's love. The more I meditate on the Word, the closer I am drawn to Him, and the more I love Him. I am not only speaking this; I feel an amazing love for the Lord. He is my light, my life, my source. He is such a big part of me.

When my daughter was about ten or eleven years old, in a vision the Lord told me, *"You are not the head of the family but I AM. This family is not just you and your daughter,* but *I AM a part of this family, and you are not the head of your daughter,* but *I AM."*

I said, "Lord, she's so young." With a finger pointing at me, God repeated His words: *"I AM the head of this family; I AM a part of this family, and I AM the head of Trisha."* I said yes Lord.

I was speaking with someone and calmly told them that I was a single parent. The Lord rebuked me and said never say that again. The Lord said, He is with me and has always been with me. I said, "Yes, Lord," and instantly felt the weight of the world lifted off my shoulder. I never realized the responsibility I felt being a parent, but God knows best. He is always there. I know that He is:

- my heart's desire

- my Saving Grace,

- the love of my life,

- my warm embrace.

It feels so good to be back in close relationship, to be part of Him, to belong to Him, knowing I am His and He is mine. "Lord, I praise You for who You are. I love and embrace You. You are absolutely wonderful. You are so very real, and your love is everlasting."

# The Prayer of Intercession

One morning as I finished praising the Lord and was about to pray for the pastor, (I was taught that when we praise the Lord, the next person to prayer for should be our pastor.) The Lord gave me someone else's name. I prayed a little and the Lord said, "not enough, pray more." I was on my knees and the Lord had me continue in prayer for the person (for maybe another thirty minutes). Whenever I praise the Lord, He would have me prayer for the same person. This continued for weeks, maybe months.

One day I said to the person, I don't know why but the Lord have me *praying for you.* She smiled and said, *"Just be in obedience and do what the Lord tells you." It feels so good when the Lord uses you.* That was my first intercessory prayer.

The Lord taught me how to intercede for others. A few months later the person called and wanted to meet with me. They seemed so nervous and said, "I think you already know the problem." I had no idea what was going on. They told me they have the AIDS virus and was believing God for a miracle. They have not been taking their medications for over a year, just trusting and believing God to heal them. Well, believe me, they got their miracle, and not because I prayed for them. God alone does miracles. God healed the person, and when they went back to be tested, no AIDS showed up in their blood. That was my first intercession. Praise the Lord for His goodness.

I will pray, "Use me, Lord, I want to be used by You. I will pray for your people to draw closer to You, for total surrender, to have a deeper understanding, a committed relationship with You. Lord, You created us in your image and love us so much."

It is hard for God to see us making the wrong decisions, drifting further away from Him. Instead of doing things our way, we should say, "Lord, have your way in me. Show me your way, oh Lord, and lead me in the path of righteousness." We need to cry out more. Let go and let God. I would recite *Psalm 51 and 91*often. "Cover me, Lord, and hide me in You. Strengthen me Lord. I need You. Help me to be strong in You always."

I was either on top of the mountain or down in the valley. Never an in-between moment. How did I get here? When did I fall? On the mountain, I was super confident. One negative thought and I would fall. I was so hard on myself. No pity, no compassion, no forgiveness. It was easier for me to forgive others than myself. My expectation for myself was too high and perfect; I could never live up to it.

In the valley it was total desperation. I cried, I groaned, I was miserable. No peace, no comfort, no rest, no mercy. I felt I had lost my mind. To some, I seemed strong because they could not see the inside and I didn't let them know. Who would want to be associated with someone who seems so crazy? The negative thoughts were destroying me. I could not help myself, and I couldn't trust anyone to tell them. My friends would pour out their troubles to me, but I kept mine to myself. They would ask for prayers, calling me at all hours. I felt my situation was worse than theirs and they could pray for themselves, but I prayed for them, because the bible says to prayer for one another. I tried to encourage them to prayer for their selves, telling them that the Lord would like to hear from them.

I would wake up with a song of praise. I printed the words and sang it all day, every day until the Lord changed it. Those songs brought much joy and peace. Praise and worship is a big part of me. It kept me in the presence of the Lord. Those songs are for healing the body and mind. Whatever I was doing, be it the dishes, laundry, cleaning, I would be worshiping the Lord. Keep songs of praise and worship on, you'll feel the difference.

An Apostle told me to listen to songs about the Blood of Jesus. She encouraged me to play those songs constantly. I found 500 Songs compiled on the Blood of Jesus. I would play the songs day and night, whether at home or not, I kept the music on. Those songs saturated the atmosphere with the presence of Jesus. There was nothing wrong with the home, I needed to shift my mind on the things of Jesus and feel his presence. Those songs plays for 8 hours and them they start over again. They were faith-building and comforting song.

When I was going through my own health crises. I could not understand how I am praying for others, and I am not healed, but I was reminded of Paul in the Bible when he sought the Lord three times about the thorn in his flesh, that it might depart from him. *"And he said unto me, 'My grace is sufficient for you, for My strength is made perfect in weakness.'" (2 Cor. 12:9).* I applied the text to myself and continued.

I did not know who to talk to about my situation, even though it was destroying me on the inside. I finally confided some things to a love one. Once spoken, the situation had no more control over me. I felt so much better, so relieved, and it was in our communication that I realized the problem was not bad. (Remember I was always harder on myself.) You are holding on to something that is no good for you, feeling ashamed, but once you let it go, it is gone. That is what the enemy does. He makes us doubt our own self-confidence, but we have nothing to worry about once we let go of the problem. We must use our faith to rise to a higher calling. That is why we should always pray for one another. In *James 5:16*, it says, *"Confess your faults one to another, and prayer one for another, that ye may be healed. The effectual fervent prayer of a righteous man availed much."*

Depression is warfare and one of the worst kinds. *Ephesians 6:10–12* says, *"Finally, my brethren, be strong in the Lord and the power of his might. (Put on the whole armour of God, that you will be able to stand against the wiles of the devil "or we wrestle not against flesh and blood, but against principalities, against powers, against the rulers of the darkness of this world, against spiritual wickedness in high places.) Wherefore take unto you the whole armour of God, that you may be able to withstand in the evil day and having done all to stand"*

My daughter said that I am strong. I said I don't think so. She said, "I watched you and no matter what you were going through, you never let go, never gave up." I told her how awful it was for me. What she saw and what I felt were two different things. I told her in those depressing moments if I had a gun, I probably would have ended it all. So glad I did not have one. On the inside, I was crying out so loud yet not a sound came out of my mouth. I put on such a brave face. It was pride. Don't let pride cause you to fall. The bible says that pride cometh before a fall.

Now I use my experience to encourage others not to keep their burdens to themselves. Let it go. Seek professional help. Find a therapist or even speak with your doctor. Don't think you are the only person that this is happening to. Seek prayers, there are many prayer groups you can reach out to.

When the joy, the laughter, and enjoyment came back, I was so thankful that I did not do the unthinkable. I have learned not to hold on to pain, weakness, rejection, emptiness, brokenness, or anything that is not of the Lord. Jesus is love, peace, joy, and if it is not from Him, you nail it to the cross. It does not belong to you. Enjoy the spiritual gifts, call on Him, speak life, quote the Word.

"You are of God little children, and have overcome them, because greater is He that is in you, than he that is in the world" (1 John 4:4).

A friend called, saying they needed to take a vacation and how bad they had been suffering from depression. They tried telling me before by giving small hints, hoping I would read between the lines. Depression strips you of your identity. It makes you feel bad, naked, alone, afraid, empty and ashamed.

You are crying on the inside, but no one knows (unless you tell them) because you cover it up so good. All the while you are tormented on the inside.

A few friends confessed that they also suffer from depression. It is a nasty, uncomfortable spirit. Don't seem to know what causes it to attack. It feels like you are fighting a losing battle and out of control. That is a deep mental illness that causes sickness in the body. *"Do not be afraid nor dismayed because of this great multitude, for the battle is not yours but the Lord"* (2 *Chron. 20:15).*

The Bible says, *"He that hath no rule over His own spirit is like a city that is broken down and without walls. (Prov. 25:28).* That scripture would sting like crazy.

You are fighting this battle, and someone pours cold water on you. You are trying to get strong and get a grip, but you can't find your way or anything to hold on to. You are trying to climb up a hill, and someone is throwing stones at you or pushing you back. You are trying to avoid being hit and lose your balance and fall.

So many times, while going through a difficult situation, the Lord would speak to me and give me a word of encouragement. I once had a vision where I was in a steel pit. Jesus came to me, held out his hand, and pulled me out. He held me close to Him and said, "I have redeemed you from the enemy. I am your Redeemer."

I also told the Lord that I felt healed but had a nagging thought that I am not worthy. I heard a voice so loud, and I look around to see who was speaking. The Lord said, "You are *worthy*." Realizing that the voice came from the Lord, I repented of my thoughts and repeated the words the Lord told me. It brought comfort to me.

One night I had a vision that an angel was speaking with me. She said to me, *"You don't even know who you are or whose you are." She told me that I am the Righteousness of God in Christ Jesus (2 Cor. 5:21).* I didn't recall hearing that scripture before, so I had to look it up in the Bible. I meditated on those words day and night and became stronger and loved myself more. That was a direct Word from the Lord of blessing and deliverance.

Note: When the Lord speaks to you and tell you something about yourself, even if you may not be feeling it, just believe. Know that God cannot lie. Man looks on the outside but God looks at the heart. God is calling you by the person that He sees. If the Lord should call you blessed, even if you may not feel blessed, just believe Him and keep reminding yourself that you are blessed.

Another time God told me, *"I love you, and you are blessed."* Imagine hearing the Lord speaking directly to you. If you ever felt like the royal, you are. That is true royalty, going from the pit to the palace.

I was about to go on vacation, and for some unknown reason, I was extremely nervous. I tried my best not to let my nervousness show. My pastor called me into her office and told me the Lord wanted me to have this word. Then she read it to me: *"And, behold, I am with thee, and will keep thee in all places whither thou goest, and will bring thee again into this land, for I will not leave thee… (Gen. 28:15).* My fears disappeared. I had a good time on vacation with my daughter and enjoyed every moment.

On our way from vacation, the plane encountered a thunderstorm. The pilot kept announcing that he had to keep going higher to avoid the turbulence. Higher and higher we went but could not avoid the storm. It felt as if we were riding on rocky terrain. My daughter was sitting next to the window. I looked out but could see only clouds. It seems as if there were snow clouds in the middle of summer. I remembered the words of the Lord when He said He will bring me back and had total peace. I had the peace that passes all understanding.

I said to my daughter Trisha, *"Look the hand of God."* In the spirit, I saw a hand holding the plane and carrying it. Instantly the presence of the Lord fell on me. She curiously looked out the window and asked, "Where is God?" I can't see Him. I could hear her voice but could not answer. That was an experience that I hope would happen again, having the presence of the Lord upon you. Thank God for giving me His promise. I didn't know why I was so nervous, but God knew. Whatever was about to happen to that plane was stopped by the presence of the Lord.

*"The angel of the Lord encamps round about those who fear Him and delivers them" (Ps. 34:7).*

In *Luke 22:31–32*, Jesus said, *"Simon, Simon, Satan hath desired to have you that he may sift you as wheat: But I have prayed for you that your faith fail not: and when thou art covered, strengthen your brethren."* I said to Jesus, "Lord, You prayed for Peter. Can you please pray for me?"

One night I was on the prayer line and a prophet told me that I would get a visitation. I had no idea what a visitation was. I thought I would be visiting somewhere. About two days after the prophet's words, I was in my prayer closet and had the visitation. The Lord said to me, *"Go ahead, you are already healed. Jesus prayed for you."* I was startled and looked around, wondering where the voice came from. Then the voice repeated itself: *"I said, go ahead. You are already healed.*

*Jesus prayed for you.*" I got up and ran downstairs and told the family. I was rejoicing and felt so much love. I smiled, laughed, cried, rejoiced, and was delighted at hearing such good news.

I started meditating more often. God said to remind Him of His promises. I took His word seriously. I often remind the Lord that He told me *I was already healed. Jesus prayed for me.* "Lord, You said it. I believe it. I believe that I am physically, mentally, emotionally, and spiritually healed in Jesus's name." This came about when I read what Jesus said to Peter.

The Word is powerful. I would feel such relief and be in control. I constantly meditate and no longer suffer from depression. It was not easy but I was determined to overcome it. Jesus said rebuke the enemy and he will flee. Remember Jesus Christ is your Lord and your God. He is in control of you, so always remember who is in control.

I used to feel that I was the only person going through my situation. I know now that it was a lie from the enemy. He seeks to control your mind and make you feel so alone. Hearing others speak of going through depression, I realize I was not alone. Now I pray for them and encourage them in the Word and meditation. Play gospel music about the blood of Jesus and saturate your surroundings with His presence.

# Mother's Diagnosis

When my mother was first diagnosed with memory loss, it was devastating. She entered the hospital with thrombosis (inflamed blood clot) in her leg. They kept her for two weeks, and when she came home, we soon realized that something was wrong. She was becoming more and more confused. I went to the hospital to speak with the doctor who oversaw her. He took me aside and said some patients on that drug usually develop memory problems, but the memory comes back in six months. (A lie from the doctor trying to cover themselves.) She just got worse.

The doctor asked me if she ever fell or sustain blows to the head. He said her MRIs showed that she did not have Alzheimer's but seemed as if she had suffered blows to the head. He said the brain did not show any shrinkage, as it is accustomed in Alzheimer's, and thought her memory loss was physical and not mental. My argument was her brain was fine when she came in the hospital and, in two weeks, there was so much damage.

Facing a crisis like this called for prayer. The more I prayed, the stronger I got. I felt my faith was so strong it could move a mountain. I prayed constantly for mother. I anointed my mother and had ministers visit my mom and prayed for her. I could not accept her condition and was determined to see her healed and enjoying life. I felt she had lost so much time in that bad marriage; and now was her chance to be happy, to travel, to do the things she loved. Her illness caused me to look to the Lord more, to depend on Him and grow strong in Him, for I believed that she would receive a miracle.

My mother was fifty-nine years young when she first showed signs of memory loss. It was a long, slow battle with me failing to give up. Taking care of her, along with my sister was a task. We held her as she cried and knew in our hearts we were giving back the love and care she so deserved. It was not an easy task but it was a true time to give. In Acts 20:35 Jesus said it is more blessed to give than to receive. We learned it's not about giving money or material things but out love, our care, out time. It is about putting others first and making a sacrifice. Before, treating Alzheimers was not as advance as it is today, and the doctors were not sure on how to treat it.

She died at seventy-nine, two weeks before her eightieth birthday. I felt so numb with the pain that I could not cry. Watching her through the years should have prepared me, yet I could not accept it. I kept telling myself that she deserved so much more. I felt as if I had let my mother down. I questioned my faith, wondering if we had done everything we could. In my praying for my mother, I never asked the Lord for His will, I just asked Him to heal her.

Then the negative thoughts came. The enemy kept saying that God did not love me, that's why He didn't heal my mother. "You prayed that your brother would live, and he died. You prayed that God would stop your father from hurting your mother, and He did not. You prayed that God would give your mother a miracle, and He did not. Look at how much you prayed, and nothing happened."

I kept quiet and tried to defend the situation as best as I could. The more I defended, the more the enemy persisted. I felt I was losing my faith to hold on to God and it seemed I was failing fast.

I started questioning the Lord why didn't my mother recover. "Lord, You said that '*if we ask anything according to His will, He hears us*' *(1 John 5:14).* '*Whatever you ask for in prayer, believe that you have received it, and it will be yours*' *(Mark 11:24)."* I did not understand. I was looking for answers, but my attitude was so very wrong. My relationship with the Lord was the most precious thing that I had, and by questioning and doubting Him, I had destroyed it. I was ashamed, and for a long time did not feel worthy of His love. I had let go of His hand. My confidence was shattered, and I had hurt Him. I could not forgive myself and could not tell anyone about what I was going through.

The worst part was to hide it and pretend that all is well. When your best friend or love one deceive you, it hurts all over, and when you hurt the one who loves you, it hurts more. Either God was punishing me, or I was punishing myself. I was expecting so much from myself that there was no room for mistakes. Even though I felt forgiven, I quoted the scriptures continually, making sure that I did not repeat the mistake.

*Psalm 51:10–12 says, "Create in a clean heart, O God; and renew a right spirit within me.* **Cast me not away from thy presence; and take not thy holy spirit from me Restore unto me the joy of thy salvation; and uphold me** *with thy* **free spirit***"*

I cried, prayed, ask forgiveness, repented, fasted—anything that could help me. Then Jesus spoke to me and reminded me that He is my Redeemer and has redeemed me. To hear His voice, hear Him call my name, to be comforted in His love was wonderful.

Redeemed:
   a. compensate for the faults or bad aspects of something/someone.

b. gain or regain possession of (something/someone) in exchange for payment.

I found much peace in Psalm 23. I studied it constantly and wrote in it on index cards and carried them everywhere. I separated the verses focusing on my needs; had file cards typed up; and put them everywhere, some in my pockets, coats, bags, wallet—everywhere. One night I had a vision of a big, tall angel dressed in white sheets came into my room and asked what was in my pocket. I pulled out an index card with Psalm 23 where specific words were underlined. The angel read the card and said, "This is good." He put the index card on the bed and left the room. I hastily got out of bed and followed to let him out the door, but he disappeared.

Coming back into the room, I picked up the index card from where the angel had put it, got in bed, and went back to sleep. When I awoke, I realized what happened. There was such a peace and tranquility in the room. I felt the presence of the Lord. I prayed, sang, dance, and jumped for joy. It was a new beginning, another second chance, feeling good, confident, whole, and reassured.

In speaking with my daughter and relating how my relationship with God was like a roller coaster, she said that I compare my relationship with Jehovah (God the Father) and my paternal father (Daddy). I listened intently to what she had to say. I had much changing to do. There were two fathers in my life: one spiritual and good and the other earthly. There is no comparison between the two fathers.

I had to look at my relationship with my father (Daddy), his disrespect and abuse of the family; how I resented him for how he treated us, always cursing and threatening us; how I blame God for not protecting us from his anger.

I knew the root cause of my depression started with my father. I lived in a house with him and was so afraid of him. I allowed my fear to control me. It became worse when I could not forgive him. I carried my bitterness, unforgiveness, and resentment with me wherever I went.

A friend of the family once asked me why my uncles didn't put a beating on my father for the abuse of their sister, to teach him a lesson and to let him know what it feels like. I told the man I always wondered the same thing.

When the Lord first told me to forgive my dad, I said I could not. I asked the Lord if He knew what my dad did. It did not matter to God because we are supposed to walk in love and forgiveness. My stubbornness and disobedience cost me much pain and suffering. It was a lesson to learn and a hard price to pay.

I finally forgave my father. While vacationing with us, we had a one-on-one. I got to pour out some of what he did and the awful things he said to us. My father cried and kept saying how sorry he was, and he asked for forgiveness. I was hurting so bad. I told him I forgive him and that I was sorry also, sorry for all the years of not talking with each other. I had to face him. I felt we had lost so many years through stubbornness and pride.

Although I forgave my father, I was still fighting his demons. Dead and gone, the memories of my childhood living with him and my mother haunted me. I would cry out to God to take them away. "Lord, I don't want to deal with this anymore." I had to learn and apply the Word of God to my situation. I saw myself nailing the past to the foot of the cross. I did it repeatedly to where it no longer affects me.

The easiest way was to give it to Jesus. Forgive and let it go as soon as possible. Bury the past and be free.

God is my strength and shield, and He has become my strong tower. I have grown to love Him, to trust Him, to know that I am His and He is mine. I feel so loved and protected. I adore and cherish being in His presence. He truly is a *good* and *loving God*. My faith in Him is growing steadily. He is my God, my Lord, my Abba Father, my Husband, my Maker, my Creator, my Redeemer, my Rock, my First Love, my True Love, my everything. I know that I cannot live without Him, for He is a part of me. The Lord explained this to me:

Jesus in God and God in Him (Jesus) and Jesus in us. The Lord said that He (God) is in Jesus and Jesus is in me, so God is inside me. Now you know that God is inside of you, you do not have to go searching miles for Him. No matter how difficult it gets, I am now in a place that I know that I will not let go of God's hand.

# My Healing, Deliverance & Restoration

On a Prayer Line one night, the Prophetess told me that the Lord said He will restore me. He will make all things new again. I was excited and expected it to happen instantly, but it did not happen overnight. I had to learn to wait and trust the Lord. (You know our time is not his time.) It was in the trusting and waiting that my healing and deliverance happened. I would constantly remind the Lord of his promise. *(Isaiah 67:6 Amp. Put the Lord in remembrance of His promises, keep not silent.)* Isaiah 43:26 KJV God said to Put Him in remembrance. Lord, I'd say, I take You at your Word. Your Word cannot lie and You Lord cannot fail.

God loves when we have conversations with Him, so go in faith and humble ourselves before Him. The pain and rejection of the past is gone. God did it. He is truly our Redeemer.

A pastor friend of mine preached a powerful message he said was for the church. (the subject **"God wants us to TURN"**

Grace and Peace to you "the intent of this word is to provoke our hearts to remember that no matter what it looks like, if we turn back to God with our whole heart, He is well able to turn any situation we face around."

### By: Pastor Richard P. Martin

The message was so powerful, I was in awe as I listened to it repeatedly. It was life changing. I wanted that word to fill my belly. The Word says "out of the belly shall flow rivers of living water." After three days of constantly listening to that message, I heard a voice say to me *"I AM A CHILD OF THE MOST HIGH GOD."* That was the Lord reminding me of who I am and whose I Am. If I face any challenges, I simply remind myself of the Word within and tackle any problem. Where I am now is so far from where I used to be. I am constantly thanking God for his goodness and reminding Him of where He's bought me from, and where I am now. It is a joy ride compared to where I used to be.

The painful years are gone. The wilderness years are gone. Gone are the days of the roller coaster, the ups and downs, the frustrations, the insecurities, the desperate times. I am in a Faith Walk. In it, you don't walk alone, you're never alone. Your walk is secured in Christ for you know who you are and whose you are.

I can only compare my relationship now to having a precious diamond that you lost. You searched diligently until you found it, and once found, you keep it close to you heart so as never to loose it again. My relationship with the Lord is the most treasured and precious thing that I've ever wanted.

# What I have Learned

I have learned to trust God. To believe in Him no matter what my situation looks like. I keep my eyes on Him and put my life in His hands. I have learned no one can love me the way that God loves me, be it mother, father, brother, sister, husband, wife, son, daughter, grandparents, friend. I never want to feel apart from Him. I cherish the closeness, the intimacy, the warm embrace, the fellowship, the love, and the security. My desire to please Him is great.

God is God and always will be God. No one can replace Him. His love is immeasurable (too large, extensive, or extreme to measure), and He is forever in us. God is the only true, holy, real, loving, living, faithful, good and perfect Father; and we can depend on Him. He keeps His promises. I can only encourage anyone to aim for a personal relationship with Him. You can talk to Him, cry before Him, walk with Him, and worship Him anytime.

You go the Father through Jesus His Son, and there is no better one to tell your troubles to, for He said in His Word, He will never leave you nor forsake you. He is with you always. Take heart my friend, for there is no greater friend you can have than Jesus the Christ. He is a Good God, our God, our Abba Father, our King of kings, our Lord of lords, our Creator, our Maker, our Restorer, our Healer, our Provider, our Redeemer, our Shepherd.

I know that God is...

- *In me* - Greater is He that is in me than he that is in the world (*1 John 4:4*).

- *On me* - The Lord is on my side; I will not fear. What can man do unto me? (*Ps. 118:6*).

- *For me* - If God be for us who can be against us. (*Rom. 8:31*).

- *With me* - The Lord will not leave you nor forsake you, He will be with you always. (*Deut. 31:6*).

- *Over me* - The Lord watches over me now and forever (*Ps. 121:5*).

- *Covers me* - God covers me with His feathers (*Ps. 91:4*).

- *Keeps me* - God keeps me under His wings (*Ps. 91:4*).

- *Upon me* - The Spirit of the Lord is upon me

- (*Isa. 61:1*).

- **Answers me** - In my distress I called to the Lord, and He answered and set me free (*Ps. 118:5*).

- **Delivers me** - God delivers me from all evil (*Matt. 6:13*).

- **Orders my steps** - The steps of the righteous man are ordered by the Lord (*Ps. 37:23*).

- **Delights in me** - God deliver me because He delighted in me (*Ps. 149:4*).

- **Loves me** - For God so loved the world that He gave His only begotten son that whoever believes in Him should not perish but have everlasting life (*John 3:16*).

- Jesus **died for** me, and I *live for* Him.

- Jesus **lives in** me and I *live in* Him.

Father Lord, I know that You are the Only, True, Holy, Righteous, Living, Good and Perfect God. You are the First and the Last. You are Alpha and Omega, the Beginning and the End. Amen.

# The grandchildren, their relationship with God:

*Jasmine* (six years old): "God is good, and I love Him. I know He will always be on my side, and I know He loves me too."

*Joyanne* (nine years old): "*God is amazing.* He is great. He will always be with me and in my heart. I will go through hard paths, but I know that He loves me and will be with me."

*LeLani* (twelve years old): "I believe in God, but sometimes the world makes me have doubts. I know God will always be there for me and I love Him. I don't hear from Him, and it confuses me, because I don't have a strong relationship with Him."

*Josiah* (sixteen years old): "I absolutely love God and know He loves me beyond measure. It amazes me with how forgiving God is. No matter how many times we sin, God will forgive us. That's astonishing because we humans will sin a lot.

*Olivia* (seventeen years old): 'God is the reason I breathe every day. He is the reason I have clothes on my back and shoes on my feet. He keeps me humble and forever grateful. I love God with everything in me. I will never forget what God has done for us. Amen."

# My Prayer for you

My prayer for you is to let go and let God. Let Him restore and heal you of your past and your present. No matter who or what you feel is responsible, let go and let God.

I hope you **love** again

I hope you **laugh** & **laugh** & **laugh**


I hope you **sing** again

I hope you **dance** & **dance** & **dance**

with ..............Jesus.

9 781637 281420